BRAVE HARRIET

The First Woman to Fly the English Channel

MARISSA MOSS

ILLUSTRATED BY **C. F. PAYNE**

Silver Whistle

HARCOURT, INC. • San Diego   New York   London

www.harcourt.com

Photograph of Harriet Quimby on p. 32 © Ullstein Bilderdienst

Silver Whistle is a trademark of Harcourt, Inc.,
registered in the United States of America and/or other jurisdictions.

Library of Congress Cataloging-in-Publication Data
Moss, Marissa.
Brave Harriet: the first woman to fly the English Channel/Marissa Moss; illustrated by C. F. Payne—1st ed.
p. cm.
"Silver Whistle."
Summary: The first American woman to have received a pilot's license describes her
April 1912 solo flight across the English Channel, the first such flight by any woman.
1. Quimby, Harriet, 1875–1912—Juvenile literature. 2. Women air pilots—
United States—Biography—Juvenile literature. 3. Aeronautics—Flights. 4. English Channel.
[1. Quimby, Harriet, 1875–1912. 2. Air pilots. 3. Aeronautics. 4. Women—Biography.]
I. Payne, C. F., ill. II. Title.
TL540.Q496M67 2001
629.13'092—dc21   99-50463
ISBN 0-15-202380-1

First edition
A C E G H F D B
Manufactured in China

The illustrations in this book were done in mixed media.
Display lettering by Tom Seibert
The text type was set in Hoefler Text.
Color separations by Bright Arts Ltd., Hong Kong
Manufactured by South China Printing Company, Ltd., China
This book was printed on totally chlorine-free
Nymolla Matte Art paper.
Production supervision by
Sandra Grebenar and Ginger Boyer
Designed by Lisa Peters

To Anne, daring to soar

—M. M.

To my family, friends, and teachers for their loving care.

—C. F. P.

It's a strange thing to see an aeroplane fly. The thing is so gawky and bumbling on the ground, so spindly and flimsy-looking, but then, once in the air, it soars with the grace and beauty of a hawk, strong enough to lift a person high above the trees and into the clouds.

I hadn't grown up wishing to be a pilot, because there were no planes when I was a girl, but once I saw one, I knew where I belonged—there, at the controls, with blue sky all around me. The day I saw my first plane was the same day I started flying lessons, eager for my chance to be alone in my own great bird.

My friends thought I was crazy. There I was, already a successful newspaper writer. Why would I risk my life in such a rattletrap, gum-and-spit contraption? But to me, there was no reason to be afraid, only a reason to soar, a longing to be among the first high up in the clouds.

And that first time I flew solo, it was as if I had finally found where I belonged. I didn't have to think about what to do, my body just knew. It was like I'd grown wings from my shoulders, flying felt so natural.

But it didn't seem natural to the licensing board when I applied for my pilot's license.

"No woman has ever received a license to fly," the official told me gruffly.

"You mean, no woman has *yet*," I replied. I went on to pass not one but two flight tests—cutting figure eights perfectly around two test pylons. And, I admit, it was very satisfying to see that official's face again as he handed me my license.

The next day, I was already flying air shows. Barnstorming, we called it, doing loop-the-loops, wing walking, and flying around Staten Island by the light of the full moon. But it wasn't enough. I wanted more. That's when I decided to do it— to become the first woman to fly solo across the English Channel.

Now even other pilots thought I was crazy. Gustav Hamel,
who had flown the Channel himself, didn't think I could do it.

"Harriet, dear," he said—but I didn't feel very "dear" at all—
"this foolishness could be the death of you. It's beastly cold,
you'll see nothing but blasted fog, and you'll only have a compass
to guide you."

"I am not afraid," I said calmly. "And I have a good compass."

"But you understand that if you're off by a mere five miles,
you'll end up over the North Sea and never be heard from
again? It happened to a fellow just a few days ago."

"I can use a compass," I insisted.

Gustav frowned and looked at his shoes, but he didn't give up. "Look here," he persisted, "you can have the glory without the danger. Here's my plan: I'll dress in your purple cloak and hood, so no one can see my face, and pretending to be you, *I'll* fly the Channel for you. We'll meet in France, switch clothing and places, and you'll fly the short bit to Calais to be greeted with a hero's welcome."

I couldn't imagine a worse course of events. "A hero's welcome for a fraud! No, thank you! You may be worried about what I can do, but *I'm* not."

And that was the last time that Gustav tried to stop me. My mind was set on what I had to do, and even he could see that. Instead, he came with me to Dover to see me off.

Monday, April 15, 1912, was the day set for my flight, but as the sun dawned, the wind gusted and the sky churned with rain clouds. My little aeroplane would have been torn apart like a kite. So I waited and waited and wondered—was I doing the right thing?

By dawn the next day, the skies were clear and calm, and I felt as sure as ever that I could do this, I could hang suspended between air and water, and it would feel right. I just knew it.

Before I got into my plane, Gustav handed me a hot-water bottle to tie around my waist.

"Remember, it's cold up there," he said, frowning.

"Thank you, Gustav." I smiled. "I can't wait to find out for myself."

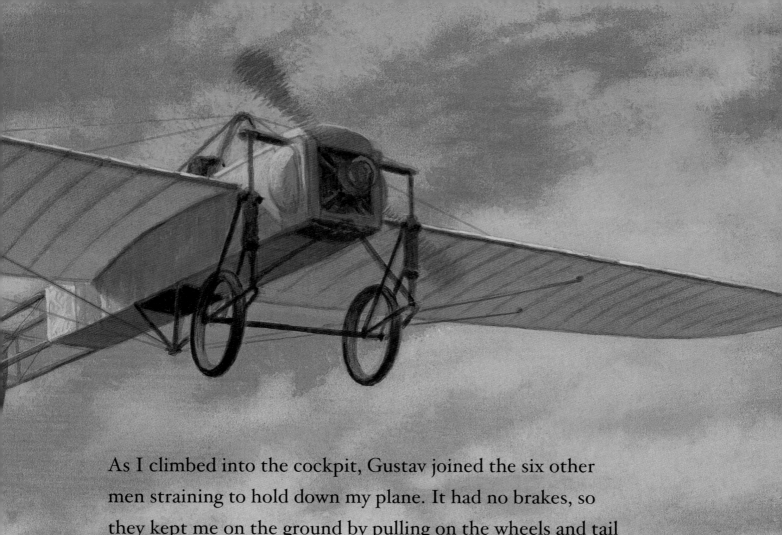

As I climbed into the cockpit, Gustav joined the six other men straining to hold down my plane. It had no brakes, so they kept me on the ground by pulling on the wheels and tail while I started the engine. I adjusted my goggles, held my compass tightly, and gave them a thumbs-up. The men let go, and the plane bumped into the air. I was off!

At 5:35 A.M. my plane left England's soil, heading over the cliffs of Dover, across the Channel, and on to France.

It was my first time to fly by compass. It was my first time to fly over water. And it was my first time to cross the English Channel. The crossing was all I had imagined it to be—the blue overhead, the blue beneath, the blue all around. Below me I could see a tugboat full of reporters following my path. Then they disappeared as I was wrapped in a thick mist. The blue was gone, and there was nothing to see but white—a cold, wet whiteness like the foam of a wave.

By 6:00 my goggles had clouded up, so I pushed them up on my forehead. Without them, I still saw only whiteness. I should have been terrified, but, oh, it was so beautiful—as much a part of flying as being in the vast, clear blue. And I had my compass to guide me. All I had to do was follow the path east and trust my plane to do the rest.

By 6:30, however, I was so cold I could scarcely feel my own hands. The white fog had crept into my bones, and I worried I would not stay alert and so would miss my compass heading. The plane suddenly lurched, and I was all sharp attention again. Something was wrong!

The plane was tilting sharply, and the steep pitch caused the engine to misfire. The motor began to sputter. There was no time to think, only time to act. I lowered the plane as steadily as I could, hoping to pancake onto the water with a gentle landing.

But just as suddenly as the trouble had begun, the sparking stopped and the motor again purred smoothly.

And now, below the clouds, I could see the coast of France.

My fingers still numb with cold, my heart still pounding from the sparks, I didn't even look for Calais but brought the plane to land on the sandy beach. It was all over so quickly. It was scarcely 7:00 A.M., and I had come so far!

A crowd of French fishermen and their families rushed over to greet me, the great fish fallen from the sky. The women hoisted me aloft once again in triumph, while the men pushed my plane up the beach, away from the rising tide. It was a wonderful welcome. Best of all, one fishwife set up a table, right there on the beach, and sat me down to a good, hot cup of tea. As I warmed my hands around the wide, thick steaming bowl, I could see the headlines already: AMERICAN WOMAN FLIES OVER THE CHANNEL!

And it might have been so, it truly might have been, but it was April 16, 1912, and for that day—and for days afterward—there was other news that eclipsed mine.

But it didn't matter, because I knew I had done it. I'd had my time in the clouds, my time surrounded by blue, and that was enough for me.

Author's Note

This story is based on the life of Harriet Quimby, the first American woman to receive a pilot's license and the first woman to fly solo across the English Channel. The descriptions of her flight are taken from the newspaper article she wrote about it as a reporter for the *New York Herald*. When Harriet made her flight in 1912, the "aeroplane" was still young as a machine, a wooden open-air contraption that looked about as strong as a good box kite. More than a decade would pass before planes would have the enclosed metal cockpits that we associate with Amelia Earhart and Charles Lindbergh. But there already existed a breed of daredevil pilots, and Harriet was among them. She made a name as an exhibition flier, performing for the inauguration of the president of Mexico in 1911, then setting her sights on crossing the English Channel.

Gustav Hamel, an early aviator who had already successfully crossed the Channel, did actually offer to trade places with Harriet, so convinced was he that the flight was beyond a woman's ability. Harriet proved him wrong, and she worked hard to promote commercial aviation and a place for women within it. She even foresaw a day when passengers would regularly be carried on flights of fifty or sixty miles!

Unfortunately for Harriet, her landing in France coincided with the news of the sinking of the *Titanic*. The newspapers were filled with news of the tragedy, and Harriet's feat didn't even make the back pages of the *New York Herald*. She was determined to keep flying, however, and died doing what she loved, soaring into the blue. The *Boston Post* wrote of her death: "Ambitious to be among the pathfinders, she took her chances like a man and died like one." Her gravestone expresses that daring as well: THERE IS NO REASON TO BE AFRAID.